LOOKING INTO THE PAST:
PEOPLE, PLACES, AND CUSTOMS

Greetings of the World

by

Richard Kozar

Chelsea House Publishers

CHELSEA HOUSE PUBLISHERS

Editor-in-Chief Stephen Reginald
Managing Editor James D. Gallagher
Production Manager Pamela Loos
Art Director Sara Davis
Picture Editor Judy Hasday
Senior Production Editor Lisa Chippendale
Designer Takeshi Takahashi

First Printing

1 3 5 7 9 8 6 4 2

Library of Congress Cataloging-in-Publication Data

Kozar, Richard.
Greetings of the world / by Richard Kozar.

   p.   cm. — (Looking into the past)
Includes bibliographical references and index.
Summary: Compares greetings used in twenty-five countries
a century ago with the salutations, gestures, and customs one
would expect to observe today.

ISBN 0-7910-4680-X
1. Salutations—Cross-cultural studies—Juvenile literature.
[1. Salutations. 2. Manners and customs.] I. Title. II. Series.
GT3050.K69 1997   97-26612
395—dc21   CIP
                                          AC

CONTENTS

CONTENTS

Culture, Customs, and Rituals

The important moments of our lives—from birth through puberty, aging, and death—are made more meaningful by culture, customs, and rituals. But what is culture? The word *culture,* broadly defined, includes the way of life of an entire society. This encompasses customs, rituals, codes of manners, dress, languages, norms of behavior, and systems of beliefs. Individuals are both acted on by and react to a culture—and so generate new cultural forms and customs.

What is custom? Custom refers to accepted social practices that separate one cultural group from another. Every culture contains basic customs, often known as rites of transition or passage. These rites, or ceremonies, occur at different stages of life, from birth to death, and are sometimes religious in nature. In all cultures of the world today, a new baby is greeted and welcomed into its family through ceremony. Some ceremonies, such as the bar mitzvah, a religious initiation for teenage Jewish boys, mark the transition from childhood to adulthood. Marriage also is usually celebrated by a ritual of some sort. Death is another rite of transition. All known cultures contain beliefs about life after death, and all observe funeral rites and mourning customs.

What is a ritual? What is a rite? These terms are used interchangeably to describe a ceremony associated with a custom. The English ritual of shaking hands in greeting, for example, has become part of that culture. The washing of one's hands could be considered a ritual which helps a person achieve an accepted level of cleanliness—a requirement of the cultural beliefs that person holds.

The books in this series, *Looking into the Past: People,*

Places, and Customs, explore many of the most interesting rituals of different cultures through time. For example, did you know that in the year A.D. 1075 William the Conqueror ordered that a "Couvre feu" bell be rung at sunset in each town and city of England, as a signal to put out all fires? Because homes were made of wood and had thatched roofs, the bell served as a precaution against house fires. Today, this custom is no longer observed as it was 900 years ago, but the modern word *curfew* derives from its practice.

Another ritual that dates from centuries long past is the Japanese Samurai Festival. This colorful celebration commemorates the feats of the ancient samurai warriors who ruled the country hundreds of years ago. Japanese citizens dress in costumes, and direct descendants of warriors wear samurai swords during the festival. The making of these swords actually is a separate religious rite in itself.

Different cultures develop different customs. For example, people of different nations have developed various interesting ways to greet each other. In China 100 years ago, the ordinary salutation was a ceremonious, but not deep, bow, with the greeting "Kin t'ien ni hao ma?" (Are you well today?). During the same era, citizens of the Indian Ocean island nation Ceylon (now called Sri Lanka) greeted each other by placing their palms together with the fingers extended. When greeting a person of higher social rank, the hands were held in front of the forehead and the head was inclined.

Some symbols and rituals rooted in ancient beliefs are common to several cultures. For example, in China, Japan, and many of the countries of the East, a tortoise is a symbol of protection from black magic, while fish have represented fertility, new life, and prosperity since the beginnings of human civilization. Other ancient fertility symbols have been incorporated into religions we still practice today, and so these ancient beliefs remain a part of our civilization. A more recent belief, the legend of Santa Claus, is the story of a kind benefactor who brings gifts to the good children of the world. This story appears in the lore of nearly every nation. Each country developed its own variation on the legend and each celebrates Santa's arrival in a different way.

New rituals are being created all the time. On April 21, 1997, for example, the cremated remains of 24 people were launched into orbit around Earth on a Pegasus rocket. Included among the group whose ashes now head toward their "final frontier" are Gene Roddenberry, creator of the television series *Star Trek,* and Timothy Leary, a countercultural icon of the 1960s. Each person's remains were placed in a separate aluminum capsule engraved with the person's name and a commemorative phrase. The remains will orbit the Earth every 90 minutes for two to ten years. When the rocket does re-enter Earth's atmosphere, it will burn up with a great burst of light. This first-time ritual could become an accepted rite of passage, a custom in our culture that would supplant the current ceremonies marking the transition between life and death.

Curiosity about different customs, rites, and rituals dates back to the mercantile Greeks of classical times. Herodotus (484–425 B.C.), known as the "Father of History," described Egyptian culture. The Roman historian Tacitus (A.D. 55–117) similarly wrote a lengthy account about the customs of the "modern" European barbarians. From the Greeks to Marco Polo, from Columbus to the Pacific voyages of Captain James Cook, cultural differences have fascinated the literate world. The books in the *Looking into the Past* series collect the most interesting customs from many cultures of the past and explain their origins, meanings, and relationship to the present day.

In the future, space travel may very well provide the impetus for new cultures, customs, and rituals, which will in turn enthrall and interest the peoples of future millennia.

Fred L. Israel
The City College of the City University of New York

CONTRIBUTORS

Senior Consulting Editor FRED L. ISRAEL is an award-winning historian. He received the Scribe's Award from the American Bar Association for his work on the Chelsea House series *The Justices of the United States Supreme Court*. A specialist in early American history, he was general editor for Chelsea's *1897 Sears Roebuck Catalog*. Dr. Israel has also worked in association with Dr. Arthur M. Schlesinger, jr. on many projects, including *The History of U.S. Presidential Elections* and *The History of U.S. Political Parties*. They are currently working together on the Chelsea House series *The World 100 Years Ago*, which looks at the traditions, customs, and cultures of many nations at the turn of the century.

RICHARD KOZAR is a former journalist, editorial writer, and weekly newspaper publisher in western Pennsylvania. He has contributed several articles on outdoor subjects to national magazines and now is a full-time writer working on various books, periodicals, and business publications.

OVERVIEW
The Greetings of the World

A s the 20th century draws to a close, it's safe to say that people communicate with one another far differently than they did in 1900. Cellular phones, facsimile machines, and the Internet allow us to pass information back and forth with people down the street or across the globe—all within seconds. Such capabilities weren't even the stuff of science fiction novels 100 years ago.

Then, business and conversations were conducted primarily face-to-face and relied as much on how something was said as on what was said. These conversations—whether about weighty subjects or the weather—all began with a greeting. Typically, the salutation was accompanied by a sign of friendliness and courtesy, which in Western cultures amounted to a handshake and slight bow at the waist. In other parts of the world, the greeting may have reflected one's status in the society, with one or both persons bowing to the other.

Certainly the world in this earlier era was a more polite, if not gentler, place. Tradition and custom required people of many countries to be at least outwardly civil to one another, even if that wasn't the way they truly felt. Looking back today, such formality may seem out of place, but that is only because we judge from our time, when greetings and speech are considerably more casual.

Still, there are countries in the world even today whose cultures require people to say more to each other than "Hi!" when they meet, and one's status, profession, or age still merit treatment that can best be described as respectful. This is a look at 25 of those countries, and the ways their people communicated a century ago and now.

ABYSSINIA.

"ENDIET ALLOO ?"

ABYSSINIA

The greeting once used by Abyssinians was fairly unusual among the world's peoples, at least in this respect: One or both hands were placed on the shoulder of the person addressed, and the speaker would say (hopefully sincerely), *"Endiet alloo?"* At least the translation is straightforward enough; it meant simply, "How are you?"

If Abyssinia doesn't ring a bell, that's because it is now known as Ethiopia, a nation in Africa that is home to more than 100 different ethnic groups, as many as 70 languages, and followers of four separate religions. It is also, in the opinion of some archaeologists, the region where the first humans appeared.

Currently, a language known as Amharic is officially recognized, as is English. Amharic is spoken by half the people in the country. And while English is not the mother tongue of choice, it is used to educate students in high schools and universities so that they will have little trouble communicating in jobs and with the world outside Ethiopia. However, as one might expect in this culturally diverse society, many Ethiopians speak more languages than these. And there is now a movement to introduce local languages in the primary grades to reflect this diversity.

If there is one constant in this often-troubled country, it is the family. This is the glue that keeps Ethiopia's different nationalities and cultures intact. Families tend to be larger here, at least in part because fewer children survive to reach adulthood in African countries.

ARABIA.

"SALAAM ALEIKA."

ARABIA

roving nomad in Arabia earlier this century would have greeted a countryman by saying, *"Salaam aleika,"* or *"Peace be upon thee,"* regardless of the time of day or occasion.

Today, the traditional greeting of Arabic-speaking men is *"issalam alaykum"* ("peace be upon you"), which would be answered by *"wa-alaykum is-salam"* ("and to you be peace"). Modern Saudi Arabia was established in 1932 after the unification of the nomadic tribes led to the victory over the Ottoman Turks. The huge oil-producing desert country is still ruled by a monarchy.

Saudis universally speak Arabic, a language inspired by both Hebrew and Aramaic. Millions of people all over the Middle East and parts of North Africa read and write in Arabic, the language of the Koran (the sacred text of the Islamic religion). Because spoken Arabic has many subtle variations, words can often be correctly translated into English in several ways. For instance, "Mohammed," Muhammad, "and "Muhamid" are all appropriate spellings for the fabled prophet and founder of Islam.

As in other Islamic cultures, Saudi men often display their friendship with one another by embracing, or even holding hands while in public. On the other hand, the same behavior between males and females would likely lead to their arrest. As in other Islamic Middle Eastern countries, public displays of affection between opposite sexes are against the law.

When a Saudi meets a stranger or foreigner, he will reveal little emotion and will likely offer a weak handshake, as opposed to the firm grip favored by Americans.

ARGENTINA.
"BUENOS DIAS. ¿CÓMO ESTÁ
VD?"

ARGENTINA

O ne hundred years ago, Argentinians tradition-
ally greeted each other with a handshake and
slight bow and spoke the same words that
would have been used in their mother coun-
try, Spain: *"Buenos dias. Cómo está Ud. (usted)?"* ("Good day.
How are you?").

Today, Spanish remains the official, and almost universally spoken, language in Argentina. It is the sole language used
by government and is what children are taught in school.
However, the evolution of Spanish into various dialects
often makes it difficult for people from Spain to understand
what is being said by people living in some areas of Argentina. In addition, Italian immigrants have created a few variations of their own: rather than say *"buenos dias"* ("good day"
or "hello!"), people near cities like Buenos Aires are more
likely to say *"buongiorno."* And "good-bye" has become
"chau," which is similar to the Italian word *"ciao."*

Argentinians are fond of talking rapidly, and they prefer
to conduct business face-to-face rather than on the telephone. As in Mexico, common practice is to proceed slowly
and graciously rather than to rush into an agreement. It is
considered impolite to end business discussions abruptly or
to discuss business during a meal.

Argentinians extend the warmth of their family lives to
friends; they hug and kiss when meeting or saying good-bye,
and they're fond of touching one another when together.
Handshakes are often exchanged between males, but hug-
ging is also common between close friends. Women either
kiss each other on both cheeks or shake with both hands.
However, in public, Argentinians generally avoid doing any-
thing to draw attention to themselves.

AUSTRIA.

"ICH KÜSSE DIE HAND."

AUSTRIA

s was the custom in the rest of Europe, greetings in Austria at the turn of the century included a handshake and slight bow. However, when meeting or departing, Austrian gentlemen also were likely to kiss the hand of a woman and say, *"Ich küsse die hand"* ("I kiss the hand").

While men still wear *lederhosen* (leather shorts) and women *dirndl* (a traditional dress) on occasion or to celebrate festivals, the rest of the time they are likely to dress in modern European fashion. Austrians will almost certainly speak German, the nation's official language, but they soften the pronunciation of their words, such as *"guten Morgen"* ("good morning"), and don't emphasize syllables as much as Germans.

And one sure way to insult an Austrian is to imply he or she is also German, or that all Austrians are alike. There are actually nine individual states in Austria, and residents of each are quick to point out how different they are.

The German and English languages have much in common, including several words with identical meanings and spellings, such as finger, hand, kindergarten, poodle, and lager, a type of beer. Other German words are so similar we can often grasp their meaning: *"Mutter"* ("mother"); *"Freund"* ("friend"); and *"Gott"* ("God").

Today, Austrians still embrace some of the formality handed down through the generations, a practice some Americans might find overdone, but one that the Austrians retain for courtesy's sake. For instance, doctors are still addressed as *"Herr Doktor"* ("Mr. Doctor").

BULGARIA.

"DOBAR DEN. KAK STE?"

BULGARIA

An outstretched hand was once the standard way for Bulgarians to greet each other, followed by the salutation, *"Dobar den. Kak ste?"* In English, the translation would be: "Good day. How are you?"

While the language remains essentially the same, Bulgarians now have gone a step further, shaking one or both hands and even passing kisses on the cheek when they greet someone. And although modern Bulgarians are often considered somewhat aloof, in conversations they frequently mix a blend of animated gestures with the spoken word. Both genders are prone to stand near each other, frequently speaking loudly and touching the other person to emphasize a point. Moreover, they often make gestures that mean the exact opposite in Western cultures. For example, among Bulgarians, shaking one's head from side to side actually signals agreement, while nodding indicates disagreement.

Students are trained to respect their elders, and this education is reflected in their speech. When greeting strangers and even former teachers later in life, they precede the person's last name with a polite Mr., Mrs., Miss, or Professor. And only when speaking with close friends, family members, or children will students use the informal version of "you."

At some point in their lives, most Bulgarians will have traveled on one of the nation's trains, which are often the scene of in-depth conversations between intimate friends as well as complete strangers. People who might not normally even greet one another elsewhere often ask about and divulge the most intimate details of their lives on a train.

CEYLON.

"AYA BOWAN."

CEYLON

I n an earlier day, the person who offered a greeting to another in this country would hold his hands together with the fingers extended. If the salutation was to a superior, the hands would be held in front of the forehead, with the head bowed. If the greeting was offered to an equal or someone beneath his or her standing, the hands would have been held in front of the body, and the person would say, *"Aya bowan,"* meaning, "May you live long."

The modern greeting still resembles the dignified custom of years before. The palms are put together at chest level and the greeter bows slightly at the waist. When greeting people of superior station, it is common practice to kneel down and bend to the floor.

This island country south of India has borne a name for practically every culture that has ruled it over the centuries. In the 18th century, Britain conquered the island and thereafter named it Ceylon, which was how it was known until 1971, when the country declared its independence and changed the name to Sri Lanka ("resplendent isle").

A language known as Sinhala or Sinhalese is spoken by 80 percent of the country's population. It draws a distinction between the person speaking and the person being spoken to. In addition, "you" can be expressed several different ways: *"Thamunnaanse,"* used for a VIP (very important person); *"Thamuse,"* a cruder term that implies disrespect; and *"Numbe,"* the expression between equals.

Sri Lankans indicate "yes" by moving their heads side to side on the diagonal, a practice also commonly seen in India.

CHINA.

"KIN T'IEN NI HAO MA?"

CHINA

The ordinary salutation among the people of China was once a ceremonious, but not deep, bow. The man would raise his clasped hands inside his spacious sleeves; the lady would bow, with her hands at her side. The common greeting was, *"Kin t'ien ni hao ma?"*, or "Today you are well?"

Nowadays, another greeting would be *"Nii hao,"* or "How are you?" "Thank you" is *"shieh shieh,"* and to say "good-bye," one would say *"tzay jiann."* Chinese has been continuously spoken longer than any other language in the world, and it is spoken by more people than any other language.

The Chinese are a polite people, often going out of their way not to embarrass someone else, even if he or she is an enemy. "No" is not a common response to a request, even if that's what the person really wants to say. The Chinese have developed a remarkable ability to disguise their inner feelings, and public displays of emotion are rare.

One practice Americans find disconcerting is the Chinese reverence for age; their way of complimenting someone is to *exaggerate* his or her age. However, their hospitality is legendary, and offending a guest is considered a major embarrassment. In China, it's also better to give a compliment than to receive one.

Every person in a Chinese household has a title, and so do outsiders. For example, children often refer to elders who are not related as *"ah yi"* (aunt) and *"shushu"* (uncle) out of respect. Brothers and sisters are never addressed by name, but by titles such as "Eldest Brother" or "Third Eldest Sister."

DENMARK.
"GOD DAG. HVORLEDES HAR
DE DET?"

DENMARK

arlier this century, the natives of Denmark, or Danes, would have greeted each other by shaking hands, bowing, and saying, *"God dag. Hvorledes har De det?"* Translation: "Good day. How have you it?"

Today, traditional Scandinavian costumes and customs are usually reserved for formal celebrations. Modern Danes are also more likely to be described as friendly, sociable, and talkative, and they tend to be casual nowadays in both their dress (teens almost all wear blue jeans) and when conversing with one another. The more formal address of *"De"* is seldom used, nor are inherited or social titles of earlier years.

Modern Danish draws freely from different languages, most notably French, German, and English. For instance, words or terms related to computers—such as hard disk—are simply borrowed from English because they have no direct translation in Danish. On the other hand, the Danes do have a word for a computer's "memory"—*hukommelse*. Terms related to cooking and the world of women's fashions have been adopted from the French, and words describing music and banking from the Italians. Second languages are also important to the Danes; over half of the people—and nearly all college graduates—speak English, since many students learn from English books and deal with English-speaking people overseas.

People from different parts of Denmark speak in three basic dialects, or variations on the formal language. However, they are gradually adopting a standard Danish called *rigsdansk* ("RIJ-dansk'), an "educated" Danish spoken by the more well-to-do natives.

EGYPT.

"NAHĀREK. SAÏD IZAYYAK ?"

EGYPT

Years ago, Egyptian men greeted each other with three handshakes, touching their heart between shakes to indicate sincerity. At the same time, they would say, *"Nahārek. Saïd Isayyak?"*, which means "Happy day. How are you?"

Like several of its neighbors, the land of the pyramids has Arabic as its national language. Arabic is spoken by over 100 million people in 17 countries. And, as in nearby countries, Egyptian men who recognize each other often use enthusiastic greetings and colorful expressions, some reflecting the religious influence of Islam on the language. For example, following a prediction by a person, such as "It will rain tomorrow," the same speaker often concludes with the phrase *"insha Allah"* ("if God wills it").

Another commonly used expression is *"maalesh,"* which means "it doesn't matter," or "things could be worse." An Egyptian man trying to maintain his dignity might say *"maalesh"* after, for example, tripping on the sidewalk. The expression is used in much the same way the French feign indifference when all doesn't go well by saying, *"C'est la vie"* ("That's life").

A typical Egyptian greeting may provoke an entire series of questions and customary responses, even though the intent may only be to say "Good morning." It could be followed, for example, by a wish for a bright, sunny morning, which in turn could be met with a wish for a bright, sunny, prosperous morning. The conversation then usually revolves around the parties' health and home life. And regardless of whether all is good or bad, the speaker typically responds that all is wonderful.

FRANCE.
"BON JOUR, COMMENT
ALLEZ-VOUS ?"

FRANCE

I n France, it used to be that men raised their hats when greeting someone, followed either by a kiss on the cheek for men or a kiss on a woman's extended hand. They would then say, *"Bon jour. Comment allez-vous?"*, which means "Good day. How go you?"

This traditional greeting remains the same even today, depending on the circumstances. For instance, to say "Good evening," the phrase changes to *"Bonsoir."* Other ways to say hello to a friend or stranger are: *"Enchanté(e),"* which means "Pleased to meet you," or *"Comment ça va,"* ("How do you do?"). "Yes" is *"oui,"* "no" is *"non,"* *"au revoir"* means "farewell," and "thank you" is *"merci."* Hands are still shaken frequently by people in the workplace and even casual acquaintances, and to be on a first-name basis with someone takes more time than in America.

Although English is commonly understood by people in France, particularly the young, who study it in school, visitors are advised to at least attempt to speak French, despite the widely held belief that natives are aloof. Outside bustling urban centers like Paris, the country's people are more likely to be considerate, patient, and well mannered. If at times they seem distant, it is only because the French love their privacy and are reluctant to invade others' unless specifically invited.

The French are also extremely expressive, relying on every inch of their faces to emphasize their words, and their hands are rarely motionless. A shrug of the shoulders means "I don't know" or "I don't care." Touching the thumb and forefinger together while raising the other three fingers means "perfect."

GERMANY.
"GUTEN TAG. WIE GEHT ES
IHNEN ?"

GERMANY

Germans would have once greeted each other with a handshake and nod of the head, or the gentleman would have lifted his hat. They would then say, *"Guten Tag. Wie geht es Ihnen?"*, which means, "Good day. How goes it with you?"

The same type of formal greeting is still likely to be heard in modern Germany, depending on the time of day. Rather than saying "Hello" or "Hi," Germans would greet someone with *"guten Morgen"* ("good morning") or *"guten Abend"* ("good evening"). To bid someone farewell, one would say, *"auf Wiedersehen,"* which literally means "or until we meet again." Friends and family members, however, would likely say the informal *"tschuss"* ("see you").

Formality is still practiced in Germany, from the use of polite table manners and shaking hands when meeting acquaintances and strangers, to the choice of greeting extended to another person. For example, it is polite to wait until a host says *"guten Appetit"* ("good appetite") before eating. And just as an American might say "Mr." or "Mrs." when speaking to someone older or someone whom they've recently met, a German would use the polite word *"Sie"* ("you") until told to do otherwise. Children also say *"Sie"* out of respect when speaking with their parents.

In business, Germans rarely call each other by their first names. Instead, the formal term *"Herr"* ("Mr."), *"Frau"* ("Mrs."), or *"Fraulein"* ("Miss") is spoken, followed by the person's last name. And professionals such as doctors are still addressed with the title *"Herr Doktor"* out of respect for their position.

GREECE.

"TI KAMNETE ?"

GREECE

The customary greeting between Greeks, who are a hospitable, handsome, and proud people, begins with a slight bow, followed by the words *"Ti kamnete?"* ("Do you ail?"). Approximately 100 years ago, when this salutation came into vogue, it was common for men in Greece to wear short, white kilts.

Greek is the oldest spoken language in Europe, having been developed 2,000 years before the time of Christ. Many scholars and poets over the millennia have been drawn to the beautiful language for its ability to depict exactly what they are trying to say. Unlike many other countries, Greece's population almost universally speaks this native tongue.

Because the Greeks are expressive physically, as well as through their language, it's no surprise that touch and gesture have an important role in communication for them. They are famous for becoming embroiled in what appear to be heated arguments with wild hand movements, but in reality, such displays of temper are routine and most times quickly forgotten. When they wave to one another, rather than use an open palm like Americans (an insult in Greece), they wave a raised index finger. And when they want to indicate "no," instead of shaking their heads side to side, Greeks snap their heads upwards.

Greek has had a tremendous influence on English, with words or parts of words frequently finding their way into our language. Examples include: *"democracy,"* which is government by the people; *"Olympics,"* athletic games held every four years in some city of the globe; *"marathon,"* a long-distance race; *"micro,"* meaning small; *"scope,"* meaning to watch; and *"tele,"* which means far.

INDIA.
"SALAAM! AP KA MIZAJ KAISA
HAI?"

INDIA

A form of greeting once used by the Mohammedans of India was with the head bent and the right hand held across the forehead, as if dust were being thrown on the head. The words that would be said were: *"Salaam! Ap ka mizaj kaisa hai?"*, meaning "Salutation! How is your health?"

People meeting in modern India would most likely refer to a god figure when speaking to one another. In northern India, for example, natives might say *"Ram Ram"* or *"Jai Ramji Ki"* ("May Lord Rama live long and protect us."). In the south, meanwhile, one might hear *"Vanakkam Swami,"* meaning "I bow to You, O Divine One!"

Men refer to each other as "brother," and to any woman they meet as "sister." Like the peoples of the Middle East, Indians also rely on facial expressions and hand gestures to convey mood and meaning. And as in Sri Lanka, the island country to the south, how one greets another in India is based on his or her status in the society. For instance, a woman meeting an elder in parts of India will bend at the waist and touch the toes of the older woman.

Today, India formally recognizes Hindi and English as its two official languages. Some 40 percent of the people speak Hindi and three-quarters understand it. However, there are also 15 separate state languages recognized, with hundreds of different dialects as offshoots. Hindi is used by people to communicate in daily life, but English also plays an important role in science and business because it's better suited for discussing technical subjects.

ITALY.

"BUON GIORNO. COME VA TU P"

ITALY

I n typical European fashion, Italians once greeted each other formally, with a bow and handshake, and said, *"Buon giorno. Come va tu?"* This means, "Good day. How goest thou?"

Today, while greeting someone no longer requires a bow, the handshake is still customary and could be followed by any of the following salutations (or *saluti*), depending on the time of day: *"Molto lieto?"* ("How do you do?"); *"Come va?"* ("How's life"); *"Come sta?"* ("How are you?"); *"Piacere"* ("Pleased to meet you"); *"Buona sera"* ("Good evening"); and, if speaking on the telephone, *"Pronto"* ("Hello").

Italy and its people have been called sensual and passionate. Romantic is another word correctly used to label the land and its inhabitants, who seem to embrace life with a zest matched by few other cultures.

Italians' zest for life is reflected in their language. Words are pronounced exactly as they are spelled and normally delivered with gusto. And if the words alone fail to convey their intended meaning, the Italian reliance on expressive gestures and pantomime almost certainly will. In one example—and a sign of the changing times—Italian women nowadays might just as easily whistle at an attractive man as the other way around.

And there's no better place to observe Italians in action than the café, where people love to meet and entertain, almost as if it were an extension of their living rooms. One topic of conversation likely to be heard in cafés around the country is soccer, the national sport and an obsession with most Italians.

JAPAN.

KONNICHI WA YOI TENKI DESU

The traditional native greeting in Japan is a bow, followed by the phrase, *"Konnichi wa"* ("This day"). This is short for *"Konnichi wa yoi tenki desu,"* which means "It is fine weather today." Different greetings and forms of expression are reserved for different times and occasions.

Manners are of great importance in Japan, and great care is taken not to offend. Even today long-held traditions remain a way of life, such as how to bow (it can depend on whether the setting is the home, the office, or when meeting overseas visitors). Etiquette is also prized—everything from proper dinner manners and selecting just the right gift for special occasions to making a gracious exit.

Unlike Americans, who often want to get to the point of a discussion in a hurry, the Japanese, one might say, prefer to "beat around the bush." Both their spoken and written sentences are thus longer because of this aversion to directness. Their entire culture revolves around communicating their intent in roundabout fashion.

The Japanese choose their words carefully, depending on the meaning they want to convey. For instance, if one wishes a youngster or playmate "to come right now," the word *"koi"* is used. But if one is being invited into someone's house or establishment, one is more likely to hear the polite invitation, *"irrashaimase."*

Like many languages, Japanese has absorbed English words. Examples include: glass—*"garasu"* for plate glass and *"gurasu"* for a drinking glass; golf—*"gorufu";* and "my car"—*"maikaa."*

MEXICO.
BUENOS DIAS. ¿CÓMO SIGUE?

MEXICO

In days gone by, Mexicans greeted each other like people the world over—beginning with a handshake. They would then say, *"Buenos dias. Cómo sigue?"*, which means "Good day. How follows it?"

By American standards, Mexicans can seem at times to be too polite. It's not uncommon for close friends who've only been apart for minutes to reintroduce themselves all over again, injecting many of the same pleasantries spoken just a short while before. While "get-to-the-point" Americans may find this practice quaint, or even tedious, it's an important ritual in Mexico.

Mexicans frequently use a greeting today that might confuse the daylights out of Americans. For example, the word *"adios,"* which we think of as simply a farewell, is also used in Mexico to greet people, regardless of the time of day. However, it is reserved for occasions when one is passing by, rather than anxious to begin a conversation.

If you don't know what time of day it is, such as during a long-distance phone call to Mexico, you can simply say *"Buenas"* and forget the second part of the expression. "Hi!" is *"hola!"* To ask how someone is, the proper expression is *"Cómo está?"* If a Mexican asks you, *"Que hay de nuevo?"* ("What's new?"), your answer would be, *"No mucho"* ("Not much"), or *"Nada"* ("Nothing").

Dozens of gestures are also used in Mexico, including pointing to one's eye, which could mean "Watch out" for someone or "Be careful," and wagging an index finger ("Cool it," or "I've had enough").

THE NETHERLANDS.

GOEDEN DAG, HOE GAAT HET U?

NETHERLANDS

Years ago, the people of the Netherlands would have shaken hands upon meeting, bowed slightly, and said, *"Goeden dag. Hoe gaat het u?"* In English, it translates to, "Good day. How goes it with you?"

Dutch, as the language is known, is still spoken throughout the Netherlands (which means low lands). Dutch has many words similar to English, such as *melk* (milk), *straat* (street), and *noord* (north). To say hello to someone today, the Dutch often just say *"hallo."* Depending on the time of day, they could also say, *"Goede morgen"* ("Good morning"), *"Goede middag"* ("Good afternoon"), or *"Goede avond"* ("Good evening").

As in most modern countries, the Dutch are more casual in their conversations and communications with each other today. However, when they meet someone for the first time, they still address them as *"Mijnheer"* (Mr.) or *"Mevrouw"* (Mrs.) followed by the person's last name. Only after the introduction has been made will they consider calling someone by their first name.

The names of several American cities are derived from Dutch, including Harlem and Brooklyn, communities in New York City. The words "cookie," "waffle," and "boss" were also contributions from the colonial Dutch settlers in New York. In addition, the people of the Netherlands have sayings similar to ours in America, including "Don't disturb a brooding hen." (Ours would be "Let sleeping dogs lie.")

Another name for the Netherlands is Holland. The country still has picturesque windmills, endless fields of tulips, and people wearing clogs *(klompen),* or wooden shoes.

NORWAY.
"GOD DAG. HVORLEDES HAR
DE DET?"

NORWAY

The Norwegian language, like Danish and Dutch, owes its origins to a Germanic language. So similar are Norwegian and Danish that both populations once greeted fellow countrymen with the same formal handshake and slight bow, saying, *"God dag. Hvorledes har De det?"* Or, in English, "Good day. How have you it?"

Today, the land that is best known to outsiders for its fjords (narrow inlets of the sea surrounded by steep cliffs) has two official forms of language: Bokmal, which reflects the strong Danish influence and is spoken in large towns; and Nynorsk, a combination of rural dialects developed in the mid-19th century.

In 1875, Finnish-speaking people made up well over half the population. Today, however, Finnish is seldom spoken. And although much of the population of Denmark and Norway is similar in appearance (fair-haired and blue-eyed), Norway—which means "far to the north"—also boasts a population of the Sami, whose shorter, dark-haired ancestors have inhabited the country for thousands of years after coming from Asia. The Sami, who occupy the northernmost reaches of Norway, have a long history of living a nomadic life based on the migrating herds of reindeer. They have their own language and customs, much as the Native Americans do in the United States. Even today, the Sami wear traditional folk dress daily—fur in winter and colorful costumes during summer—as well as during holidays. They have no words for things they are not familiar with, such as "war" or "farming." On the other hand, the Sami have almost 100 different terms to describe snow conditions.

PALESTINE.

"KEIF HĀLAKA ? "

PALESTINE

Once upon a time, the people of Palestine would greet one another by either clasping the other's right hand in his own, or, if they hadn't seen one another recently, by clasping all four hands together. Each would kiss the other on the right and left shoulder alternately, saying the words, *"Keif hālaka?"* ("How is your condition?").

Today, Palestine is not the same fertile coastal plain along the Mediterranean it was a century ago. In 1948, control of Palestine, or the Holy Land, was transferred from British rule and divided between Israel, Jordan, and Egypt. And in 1967, Israel seized control of the entire 9,000 square miles that previously comprised Palestine. Arabs, Muslims, and Jews, however, continue to live in Israel in what can best be described as an uneasy peace.

Hebrew is the official language of Israel. However, Arabic is the predominant language of Palestinian-majority towns such as Bethlehem and Hebron, and throughout the West Bank. In addition, English is spoken by both Jews and Arabs and is taught to children in schools.

Israelis are famous for gesturing when they speak. One gesture, holding the palm upward while pressing the thumb and forefinger together, means "wait a minute." They also have a saying whose literal meaning is that they "don't believe you," which can puzzle a Western storyteller. Actually, what is meant is that something is "unbelievably wonderful."

Some do's and don'ts in Israel: In some areas, women must wear blouses covering their arms and also wear dresses below the knee. Also, shaking hands or picking up food with the left hand is considered bad manners.

PERSIA.

"SALAMON ALEYKUM."

PERSIA

I n the country that until 1934 was known as Persia, people commonly greeted each other with a slight bow, followed by the expression *"Salamon aleykum,"* or "Peace be upon you."

Today, the country is known as Iran and is inhabited by many ethnic groups, including Iranians (two-thirds), Azerbaijanis, Kurds, Arabs, Turkomans, Baluchis, Jews, and the Qashqa'i, a tribe of nomads. The most commonly spoken language in modern Iran is Farsi, which was named in recognition of the people of Pars, a region in the country's southwest. Due to the influence of the Arabs, Pars became known as Fars, and thus the people's language became Farsi. Inhabitants of the region were known as Irani, which in Persian means Aryan.

Unlike most Westerners, the Iranian people often gesture to each other a great deal when conversing, using their hands and arms to make their point. In addition, their faces often telegraph their mood or meaning. To signal friendship, Iranians will hold out their arms to a person. And to signal "I'm *really, really* attracted to you," an Iranian man would turn his hand palm up and wave his index finger to a woman. However, public touching between men and women is not allowed.

As is true of many countries, the same gestures mean different things in Iran and the United States. For example, a thumbs up in the U.S. means "good job," "good luck," or "everything's fine." But in Iran, that gesture would be taken as an insult.

ROUMANIA.
"CE MAI FACI P" OR "CUM
STAI P"

ROUMANIA

The form of greeting used 100 years ago in Roumania (today Romania) resembled that used in other European countries: lifting the hat, shaking the hand, or simply bowing, depending on whom one was meeting. Then, the speaker would say, *"Ce mai faci?"* ("How do you do?"), or *"Cum stai?"* ("How are you?").

"Ce mai faci" is still used as a greeting today in Romania, but also heard is *"buna ziua"* ("hello!"). If a native wanted to learn your name, he would ask, *"Cum te cheama?"* To respond, you would say, *"Ma numesc _____"* (My name is _____). *"Da"* means "yes," the word *"nu"* means "no," and to say "please," the proper expression is *"poftiti."*

To greet someone in the morning, you would say, *"Buna dimineata."* "Goodnight" is said *"Noapte buna,"* and farewell or good-bye can be indicated by saying *"La revedere."* Another common saying in the modern Romanian tradition is *"Domnui sa te aiba,"* which means "God be with you."

One reason Italians and French can often grasp the gist of a conversation in Romanian is that all three languages have much in common with Latin. Besides being fluent in their native tongue, many young Romanians can also converse in German (spoken in the western part of the country) and English. Still, Romanian is spoken by about 90 percent of the population. The Gypsies of Romania, who travel around the country rather than live in fixed homes or locations, also speak their own language, Romany.

One of the most notorious figures in Romanian history is Vlad Tepes, a 15th-century ruler whose life provided some of the inspiration for the modern-day character of Dracula.

RUSSIA.
"ZDRAVSTVUETE KAK
POJIVAETE P"

RUSSIA

Because Russia encompasses so many different nationalities—over 100—greetings vary from region to region. In the western part of the country, people meeting one another would once have bowed, shaken hands, and said, *"Zdravstvuete kak pojivaete?"*—literally, "Hail, how do you live?"

Today, Russian greetings include: *"Zdrah'stvooite!"* ("Hello!"); *"Do'bree den!"* ("Good day!"); and *"O'chen rat s vah'mee paznako'meetsa!"* ("Pleased to meet you!").

Russian, which belongs to the Slavic linguistic family, is still the chief language of the country, since all but one-fifth of the nation's population is Russian. Words that Americans would likely be familiar with are *vodka*, an alcoholic beverage made from potatoes; the *czars*, a name for the ruling monarchs of Russia who were overthrown by the Communists early in the 20th century; and *glasnost*, the spirit of openness adopted by Russia following the fall of communism and the breakup of the Union of Soviet Socialist Republics (U.S.S.R.) earlier this decade.

Today, Russians have a reputation among outsiders for falling into two stereotypical groups: those who are open, hospitable, friendly, and generous; and those who are brooding, suspicious, conniving, and inhospitable. Much depends on the person's station in life; the "official" Russian, like a customs agent or policeman, is most likely to be the cold-hearted character. To a large degree, these officials embody the steely image of the former Soviet Union.

Meanwhile, the "man in the street"—a shop owner, a newsstand vendor, or simply a passerby—is often the epitome of a warm-hearted native, who will go out of his way to greet or help a stranger.

SPAIN.
BUENOS DIAS, ¿COMO ESTA VD.?

SPAIN

The customary greeting in Spain began no differently than in other parts of Europe—with a handshake, followed by the words, *"Buenos dias. Cómo está Ud. (usted)?"* They mean, "Good day. How are you?"

Nowadays, people may also greet each other by saying, *"Hola. Cómo te llamas?"* ("Hello. What is your name?"). Other useful Spanish words are: *"sí"* ("yes") and *"no"* ("no"); *"por favor"* ("please"); *"gracias"* ("thank you"); *"adios"* or *"hasta luego"* ("good-bye"); *"Señor"* ("Mr."); *"Señora"* ("Mrs."); and *"Señorita"* ("Miss").

Every street, café, and main square in Spain is a likely place for people to gather, gossip, and observe other people doing the same. Certain to be overheard sooner or later is a *"piropo"*—a complimentary word or expression delivered by a man to a woman he finds attractive. In response to this flirting, a woman may respond with a shy smile or a witty reply of her own.

To first-time observers, Spaniards often appear reserved, but their demeanor usually masks a warm hospitality that frequently is matched only by a tendency to be opinionated. It's been joked that if you ask five Spaniards a question, you'll receive half a dozen opinions.

One of Spain's most enduring traditions is the *"fiesta"* (also the word for "party"), a religious celebration that includes dancing in the street, processions, masquerades, and a bullfight. In Barcelona's Plaça de Catalunya, children may celebrate by dancing the *sardana,* while elsewhere in the country bulls may be running down the streets—and over males attempting to prove their courage by joining them.

SWITZERLAND.
"BON JOUR. COMMENT
ALLEZ-VOUS ?"

SWITZERLAND

witzerland is a crossroads country with people of multiple nationalities speaking four different languages: German, French, Italian, and what's known as Romansh. In the western, French-speaking region, the greeting used today, as at the turn of the century, would be, *"Bon jour. Comment allez-vous?"* Or, translated into English, "Good day. How go you?"

Even the country itself has different names: *Schweiz* (German); *Suisse* (French); and *Svizzera* (Italian). As one might expect, most people in Switzerland are multilingual, German being by far the predominant language. About 18 percent speak French, 10 percent Italian, and 1 percent, Romansh (a language developed after a native people in Switzerland were conquered by the invading Romans).

Since German, French, and Italian are the official languages, signs throughout Switzerland are routinely written in all three of them, oftentimes with English included. If that weren't confusing enough, although German is spoken by two-thirds of the population, it is not the same dialect spoken in neighboring Germany. Compounding matters, while the official German used in business and government also appears in newspapers, in books, and on television broadcasts, a different version is spoken by most of the Swiss German-speaking population.

Languages aren't the only contrasts in Switzerland. For a nation long known for its neutrality in conflicts, it has one of the most well-trained, heavily armed citizen armies in the world. And while farmers serenely raise goats on the peaks of remote alpine meadows, watchmakers in the industrial centers make timepieces with—what else?—Swiss precision.

TURKEY
"SABAH-I SHERIFLER. KHAÏR
OLSOON?"

TURKEY

Turkish men once saluted each other in military fashion and said, *"Sabah-i sherifler. Khaïr olsoon?"* The translation in English would be, "Good morning. How do you do?"

The modern Turkish expression for "good morning" is now *"gunaydin."* To say "goodnight," one would say, *"iyi geceler."* And "hello" is *"merhaba."* To say "no," a Turk could say *"hayir."* But the same meaning can also be conveyed by saying *"yok,"* which translates into "there is none."

Today, nearly everyone in Turkey speaks Turkish, with a small minority of the population speaking Kurdish and Arabic. French, English, Greek, and Armenian may also be heard in the larger cities. Several of these languages have influenced Turkish, as in the case of "thank you." While the word *"sagol"* is one way to express gratitude in Turkey, *"mersi"* is another version—and clearly one reflecting a French point of view. Similarly, the French word *"pardon"* has been absorbed into the country's lexicon and carries the same meaning: "excuse me."

As in some other parts of the world, men in Turkey regularly express friendship to one another by holding hands while walking down the street or embracing and kissing on the cheek upon meeting. These practices are simply part of the culture. But as in certain Arabic countries, these displays of social bonding are also reserved for males only. When men meet in the village coffee houses and eateries to exchange conversation, women are not welcome, and even the establishment's workers are exclusively male.

CHRONOLOGY

4000 B.C.	The first written language is developed in China.
2000 B.C.	The Greek language is developed.
50 B.C.–A.D. 450	The conquests of the Roman Empire spread the Latin language through Europe and northern Africa.
1845	Amharic becomes the national language of Abyssinia.
1866	Nynorsk form of Norwegian created to counter Danish influence on language.
19th century	English education begins in India.
1889	Denmark's government adopts nationwide spelling rules.
1928	Under the leadership of Kemal Atatürk, Turkey adopts the Latin alphabet
1938	Romansh made one of the national languages of Switzerland.
1945	Japanese government reduces number of kanji characters to 1850.
1949	Putonghua first taught in Chinese schools.
1970	English becomes the "common tongue" of business.
1975	Demotic Greek named official language of Greece.

1978   Sinhala declared official language of Sri Lanka (formerly Ceylon).

1991   Laws passed in Romania forbidding discrimination against languages. (Before 1989, the Communists in power in Romania ordered only Romanian spoken in the country.)

INDEX ✳

FURTHER READING

Cultures of the World (Series). New York: Marshall Cavendish Corp.

Fodor's (Series). New York: Random House, Inc.

Franz, Carl. *The Peoples' Guide to Mexico*. Ninth edition. New Mexico: John Muir Publications, rev. 1992.

Frommer's (Series). New York: Simon & Schuster, Inc.

Harper, Paul. *The Arab-Israeli Issue*. Florida: Rourke Enterprises, 1987.

Major World Nations (series). Philadelphia: Chelsea House Publishers.

Michelin Tourist Guide (Series). France: Michelin et Cie.

8.3/1